Other works published by the author, available from iUniverse:

A Bell Curve and Other Poems (2013)
An Artist's Model and Other Poems (2012)
Black Hole and Other Poems (2012)
Pursuit and Other Poems (2011)
Persistence and Other Poems (2010)
Celebrations and Other Poems (2009)
War-Wise and Other Poems (2009)
Surface Tension and Other Poems (2008)
Confusion Matrix and Other Poems (2007)

The Longest Month and Other Poems

DAVID J. MURRAY

THE LONGEST MONTH AND OTHER POEMS

Copyright © 2016 David Murray.

All rights reserved. No part of this book may be used or reproduced by any means, graphic, electronic, or mechanical, including photocopying, recording, taping or by any information storage retrieval system without the written permission of the author except in the case of brief quotations embodied in critical articles and reviews.

iUniverse books may be ordered through booksellers or by contacting:

iUniverse
1663 Liberty Drive
Bloomington, IN 47403
www.iuniverse.com
1-800-Authors (1-800-288-4677)

Because of the dynamic nature of the Internet, any web addresses or links contained in this book may have changed since publication and may no longer be valid. The views expressed in this work are solely those of the author and do not necessarily reflect the views of the publisher, and the publisher hereby disclaims any responsibility for them.

Any people depicted in stock imagery provided by Thinkstock are models, and such images are being used for illustrative purposes only. Certain stock imagery © Thinkstock.

ISBN: 978-1-4917-8783-0 (sc)
ISBN: 978-1-4917-8784-7 (hc)
ISBN: 978-1-4917-8785-4 (e)

Print information available on the last page.

iUniverse rev. date: 02/18/2016

Contents

Introduction ix

1. The Longest Month.. 1
2. Hope.. 3
3. Realities 4
4. A Cold End of April #1 5
5. A Cold End of April #2................................. 6
6. Old Photographs 7
7. Now 8
8. A Wall.. 9
9. Foliage 10
10. You Stand Alone.......................................11
11. May Day—May 1, 2015 12
12. Appearances—May 1, 2015 13
13. May 2, 2015...14
14. Duty—May 2, 2015 15
15. I Want To...—May 2, 2015 16
16. May 3, 2015...17
17. Words—May 3, 2015.................................18
18. People—May 3, 2015 19
19. Secrets and Lies—May 3, 2015 20
20. May 4, 2015 21
21. May 5, 2015...22
22. May 6, 2015 23
23. What Matters—May 6, 2015 24
24. May 7, 2015...25
25. A Future Time—May 7, 2015..................... 26
26. May 8, 2015 27
27. Fresh Air—May 8, 2015............................ 28
28. How I'll Write—May 8, 2015.....................29

29. May 9, 2015 30

30. Weeks, Etc.—May 9, 2015 31

31. May 10, 2015 32

32. Reading the Paper—May 10, 2015 33

33. Paperwork—May 10, 2015 34

34. May 11, 2015 35

35. May 12, 2015 36

36. Kicking Myself—May 12, 2015 37

37. A Good Guy's Lament—May 12, 2015 38

38. An Old Man's Lament—May 12, 2015 39

39. May 13, 2015 40

40. The Aga Khan Museum in Toronto—May 13, 2015 41

41. May 14, 2015 42

42. Reconstruction—May 14, 2015....................................43

43. What Hurt I've Done—May 14, 2015 44

44. May 15, 2015 45

45. Faint Heart—May 15, 2015 46

46. Sunset—May 15, 2015 47

47. May 16, 2015 48

48. May 17, 2015 49

49. Your Best—May 17, 2015 50

50. As You Were—May 17, 2015 51

51. May 18, 2015 52

52. For Reasons Purgatorial Perhaps—May 18, 2015 53

53. May 19, 2015 54

54. Straight Talk—May 19, 2015 55

55. May 20, 2015 56

56. If I...—May 20, 2015 57

57. Heat and Cold—May 20, 2015 58

58. On Death—May 20, 2015 59

59. Correctional—May 20, 2015..60

60. When I'll See You—May 20, 2015 61

61. May 21, 2015 62

62. In a Field—May 21, 2015 63

63. If Chance Be Chance—May 21, 2015...........................64

64. The Roots of Verse—May 21, 2015...............................65

65. May 22, 2015 66
66. Images of You—May 22, 2015 67
67. May 23, 2015 68
68. May 24, 2015 70
69. Permanence #1—May 24, 2015 71
70. Permanence #2—May 24, 2015 72
71. Body and Soul—May 24, 2015 73
72. This View, Again—May 24, 2015 74
73. Phone-Thoughts—May 24, 2015 75
74. May 25, 2015 76
75. At the Aquarium—May 25, 2015 77
76. The Midges Have Gone—May 25, 2015 78
77. Warmth—May 25, 2015 79
78. Memorial Day—May 25, 2015 80
79. Seeing You Again—May 25, 2015 81
80. May 26, 2015 82
81. Measurements—May 26, 2015 83
82. You Are Just Fine—May 26, 2015 84
83. In a Field Again—May 26, 2015 85
84. A Proof—May 26, 2015 86
85. Below My Balcony—May 26, 2015 87
86. Troubles—May 26, 2015 88
87. Impatience—May 26, 2015 89
88. May 27, 2015 90
89. Luxuriating—May 27, 2015 91
90. A Storm—May 27, 2015 92
91. Helping You—May 27, 2015 93
92. Tornados—May 27, 2015 94
93. The Unforeseen—May 27, 2015 95
94. A Loud and Glorious Sunset—May 27, 2015 96
95. May 28, 2015 97
96. Chores—May 28, 2015 98
97. Fate—May 28, 2015 99
98. You—May 28, 2015 100
99. Me—May 28, 2015 101
100. Us—May 28, 2015 102

Introduction

I am writing this introduction to *The Longest Month and Other Poems* on my 78th birthday. The book is addressed to a person aged 72. I have known her since the 1970s. When her husband died recently, she phoned me to tell me this. A few days later, I phoned her to ask if we could meet in the near future. She agreed, but needed to wait for some weeks before she would be free to do so. Poem 1, titled "The Longest Month," describes the course of these events.

The remaining poems were all written during this waiting period; we planned to meet at a train station on May 29, 2015. The poems are numbered in the chronological order in which they were written. From Poem 11 onward, all poems are dated; for example, Poem 11 is titled "May Day—May 1, 2015." Poem 12 was written that same day and was titled "Appearances—May 1, 2015." Poem 13 was written the following day, so is titled "May 2, 2015." This pattern of titles is maintained for the rest of the volume.

In my third volume, *War-Wise and Other Poems*, the second section had been titled One Hundred Mood Poems. These were essentially exercises in the craft of poetry writing. For *The Longest Month and Other Poems*, I set myself an analogous goal of writing exactly one hundred poems, the last to be written just prior to May 29, 2015. Poem 100 was indeed written on May 28.

In previous volumes, I have used the introduction to explain certain features of that volume that I thought might be unfamiliar to some readers. In the present volume, all the poems were written in my apartment in Toronto, whose balcony overlooks Lake Ontario straight ahead, while to the south-west a low hill constitutes the horizon before dipping down toward the shoreline of the lake. The hillside is covered with trees, between which can be glimpsed occasional rooftops of houses. The trees change colour with the seasons; as in previous volumes, the changing view of the hillside day by day is made an undercurrent; this device to ensure thematic continuity is particularly important in *The Longest Month and Other Poems*.

Some references in the text require a little explanation. In Poem 40, the Aga Khan Museum was opened to the public in early 2015; its interior includes a wonderful architectural backdrop for its exhibits of Islamic art. In Poem 75, the setting is the new Ripley's Aquarium, located in downtown Toronto; it provides superb natural aquatic backgrounds for its impressive collection of marine and freshwater wildlife. In Poem 51, "'Victoria Day'" refers to a Canadian national holiday which fell on May 18 in 2015. In Poem 78, "'Memorial Day'" refers to a national holiday in the United States, which, in 2015, fell on May 25. In Poem 47, the "biography" refers to a 1000-word summary of one's life after leaving school at about the age of 18; this summary was prepared for a class reunion to be held as part of the celebrations of the 500th anniversary of the founding of Manchester Grammar School in the U.K.

I am deeply indebted to Arvie Fernandez of iUniverse for her help in getting these poems ready for publication. I also thank Rachel Breau, MLIS, for research assistance.

1. The Longest Month

Age brings its own small regimen of loss,
Which sometimes spills its venom as pure grief;
And something like a fury tries to toss
Such feelings into limbo for relief;

Such was the case six years ago when I
Woke up one morning to an empty bed;
Esther had gone, but that was no reason why
I could not be befriended in her stead.

About five hundred months before, I guess,
We'd met a couple accidentally
Who, like us, loved books and beasts, and yes,
The husband taught psychology, like me;

They moved away, after two years or so,
To a new job in a brand-new teaching-place;
But phone calls and letters and Christmas cards would go
Unceasingly, year after year, to their address

For nearly forty years, till Esther died;
I struggled on another six alone;
But then the husband crossed to the other side;
And the wife, by way of talk and telephone

Began to ease into her widowhood.
Some days after his death, I heard from her
On an April day when I wasn't feeling good
About being an unconfirmed bachelor

A state of which I'd never been too fond
I asked to see her, if she could get away;
She acquiesced, and later, did respond
That she'd come here, but not till the end of May,

A wait of more than a month, that was; this wait
Would seem long, with time seeming slow,
Involving hours reluctant to accumulate,
Spinning, instead, their spans *adagio*;

And so I wrote a poem with no date;
It was written on an April day so cold
That Spring could only be classified as late;
But then it was that an endeavour bold

Reared up from the indecorum of my brain:
I'd write her one or more poems every day
Until we'd meet each other once again
At the end of that interminable May.

2. Hope

I see my escarpment's landscape fraught with rain
That lashes at my windows, Chanticleer
Crowing at vicious Time; but you were here,

Absent in person, but present on the phone;
Before the rain began, you spoke, and I
Felt a move immense of tumbled sky

And regal hope that life would once again
Heave and remove all tumbrils out the way
So that, with death removed, I'm free to say

All that I'd wanted to say to you alone:
That what I feel can nothing other be
Than a magnificent hope to be with thee.

3. Realities

If you, inspiratrix, be what you seem,
Then spur me out from any vapid dream
And throw realities real into a stream
Of verses that never fear to sound extreme.

4. A Cold End of April #1

Into the brightness of an onslaught day,
The coldness of the morning seems
A restful and reliable beginning.
But it's zero degrees;

The sun shines clearly and resplendently
On sloping roots and branchy arms
And a car moves slowly down a modest hill;
Its lights are on;

How trustworthy is this promise of same-day sun?
It can fold back on itself, contorting;
It can curl up, like a girl in a sun-shell's clutch;
Or not;

My frolicking with Nature as were she you
Speaks to my want to do what you want too.

5. A Cold End of April #2

I must admire what Nature does right here
When Spring abandons Winter, and the sun
Outsprays its steady path with overrun
Of light upon our heady atmosphere;

I think of you there, away, afar; I grope
At an image of a solemn courageous You
Looking at fields from the ramp that steadily drew
You both to your house-door up its steady slope;

His walking slowed as the autumn sun grew red;
And then came frost and a frivolous ice and snow
That brought you *rigor mortis* in its slow
Infilling of the footprints you'd both made;

I look at your image, then slowly turn away
To stare at the coldness that dominates today.

6. Old Photographs

Old photographs that contrast black and white
Are all we have of former eras drear;
And though a family would starve itself a bit,
They'd still finance a photo every year;

And nothing seems odd about the way they stand,
Or old about their bygone vanity;
The men stare out, their egos well in hand;
Deftly, the women display their sanity;

And you have family long pedigreed;
You would fit well, a hundred years ago,
Into a family photograph decreed
To be a modest record that would show

The unforgettability of their name;
But you, by yourself, yield the portrait I would frame.

7. Now

You're blurry, like a 1960s photo;
Come now, move into the light of Now;
Let your long youthful hair of yesteryear
Float into the world you have right here,
Where life goes on, though Nature's colours die,
And your greying hair tells truth that cannot lie.

From long-gone times, your hair has fallen loose;
Your raven hair that captured Night-time's noose
In a falling valley-sphere of youth and light
Still falls (but with less of black and more of white)
Down on your dreamy shoulders; I start to shake
When I think what a treasure it would be to take

One hand to caress the crispness of one tress
While the other retrieves the anatomy of your dress.

8. A Wall

A wall of passive rocks around a dell
Whispers to all of me how all of you
Might lie, luxurious and green, within
A wall of over-geological hardness,
Repelling visitors who only want to call;
But deep inside, you know the wall must fall.

I stand, humble and entrenched, outside
That unaesthetic rocky palisade
That you present to most, impeccably.
But you must realize that there, beyond
Your fort, lies a waiting wonderland
That you can bring to blossom with your hand;

And as you watch its foliage rise and swell,
Luxurious green on all would weave its spell.

9. Foliage

Blooms that burst through their charismatic buds
Sing eloquent blossoms of upward-burgeoning song
Of how the new world of this emphatic Spring
Mirrors the world to which I now belong
Where you are Arch-Chief and Excellency.

I do not want to move to upper heights
Where golden skies meet cataracts of sun
In a springtime spread, mosaic, to the stars;
I'd rather stay, nestled within the union
Of cup and flower that symbolize your You,

And see, through the overshading overplay
Of veined leaves and branching foliage,
How the light of the sky shades slowly into night
As darkness's mantle of black falls to engage
Your beauty and your arch bewitchingness.

10. You Stand Alone

O You, to what a depth you engulf and riddle me
With endless concoctions of all your smiling ways,
Leaving me nothing to do but surrender and crown you
With verses dispensing all shapes and all manners of praise!

You can stand alone in a field, with a darkening sky
Distilling the start of an evening smitten with cold.
Your hat is on tight, but your hair has unravelled itself
And now moves, in a flapping endeavour, to frisk and to hold,

At moment A, your neck, or, at moment B, your arm;
You stand alone; the stubble of August lies prostrate;
The earth breathes out on itself to reduce any chances
It freeze; you look out at the landscape you dominate

And see only winter; but, here, I can give you more choice;
I've told you how much I adore the mezzoish sound of your voice.

11. May Day—May 1, 2015

It's May the first, and all the willow trees
That sprinkle my hillside's eminence shine green,
Completely out of kilter with the browns
That mark those other trees still standing leafless,
Unfruitful still from winter's overtime,
And days away from what they should have been;

And here I sit with pen poised here to write
That, countering drab, those willow-greens stand out
Just as you, in my mental world of friends and kin,
Stand out as she who woke me awake today,
The First of May; her image filled my mind,
Where it was anchored by a lack of doubt;

I pray that that other 'mayday' never show
Where thoughts that came first are also the first to go.

12. Appearances—May 1, 2015

I'm getting thin, the muscles loose and spare,
Not like a ballerina's glorious arms,
Taut and smooth, so smooth I dare not speak,
But signalling age, like a woman's underchin
Or the balladic duct of an overwrinkled breast.

I must evade new nervousness and rue;
I must uphold the Chanticleer of youth,
And never spurn the offered open thigh,
But traverse, as if remorseless, open facts,
And cancel dreams to registers of nothing;

For I know how your ravishing thinness fattens me;
It lures, with its spread of smooth alluringness,
Me to the mettle of you, riveted upon
The tender pliability of your being.

13. May 2, 2015

Daylight accumulates, dimly dawning,
At six, on the hour, of the second of May;
I quietly think "what a beautiful morning"
And figure I'll quietly get work done today;

For mornings that total to twenty-seven
Stretch to the 29th of May,
And I think I suspect that "pennies from heaven"
Will muddle my songs of "where antelopes play";

So I'll bury myself in my bookworm's haven,
Eat cheaply to save for the last days of May,
Pretend to the world that "I ain't misbehavin'"
And chase any jinxes out of the way,

Till finally dawns, on May 29,
The day when your eyes might lock onto mine.

14. Duty—May 2, 2015

Twist the lissom ribbons of revenge,
But subtly, so that when you write them down,
No one can ferret out their magnitude
Or claim that you're a coward or a clown;

Hint subtly of a hidden vein of malice,
Betray a tiny taste of malignity,
And barricade with rounded words your anger,
And all the time display a dignity;

Keep hidden, if you can (but you cannot),
What vengefulness seepeth from your inner wounds,
And hide what would be howls of torrent-anguish
Beneath a lacy veil of pretty sounds;

For poets have a dreadful call to duty,
Where only the Good is stored with sonic beauty.

15. I Want To...—May 2, 2015

I want to trace new writings on the sky
That state how your many virtues stir my own,
But I'd fear unfeigned mockery from passers-by.

I want to weld great sculptures on small fields
That symbolize how your empathetic artistry
Inspires a reverence that to no one yields;

I want to build tall buildings high on the tops
Of cliffs and mountains, blazoning to the world
An admiration for you that never ever stops;

I want to play, to angel's music that breaks their hearts,
So full it is, full-panoplied, of you,
Maestro and mistress at once of the musical arts;

And if you think all this exaggerates,
So what? Too little only irritates!

16. May 3, 2015

I spread a carpet of thick marigolds
To greet the sunshine of this third of May;
There's not a cloud in this high and hopeful sky,
And after winter's furore, one asks why
A record heat should permeate today;

No cloud disturbs this high and halcyon blue;
The lake is paler blue and seems to wait
For heat to spread its hospitable change
Out to all edges of the Lakeshore's range,
Restoring what winter had failed to decimate;

We have such luck to know we'll meet when Spring
Spreads its eternity over everything,
And crocuses with petals widely splayed
Fade to give way to Summer's cavalcade.

17. Words—May 3, 2015

I trust that what's predictable will ensue
And blatant affection, built over many years,
Will give to you the credit you are due,
And I receive what's sadly in arrears,

The doting recognition I am me,
With perhaps a hint or thrust of gratitude
That you cognize my true sincerity
When I heap upon your head beatitude

For your being you, a sylph of stony rage
Supplanted by a wreath of welcome wit,
And dicta drained of subtle subterfuge,
And approbated words that you transmit

In sounds across the telephone when you
And I discuss what we might plan to do.

18. People—May 3, 2015

You—I speak of you—display
A growing affability
Which, fern-like, widens every day
With manifold sagacity
To tell me what you want to say
With unabashed tenacity.

You—I speak of women—show
Adaptions to whatever is,
But deep beneath your outer glow
You seek a future armistice
"Where men may come and men may go"[1]
But women will preserve the peace.

And I—as a man—must sigh and sit,
Worrying about the cost of it.

---

[1] A quotation from Tennyson's poem "The Brook."

19. Secrets and Lies—May 3, 2015

Lies are the arbitrage of turpitude,
But sins of omission can be perverse;
Mistrust brings a deficit of certitude,
But silent secrets are portents of worse;

So let me tell no secrets to the stars
But only to you, into your patient ear;
Old people have so very much to say
And even more, when romance counts, to fear.

20. May 4, 2015

On Monday May the fourth I was up at four;
No light relieved the sombre night-time sky;
But up I got, caught up on some reading, and ate,
And watched TV while the time slid smoothly by,

Till I was awakened from a doze by you;
The telephone rang, as did my mind, when I
Learned it was you who was there on the end of the line,
Slim, svelte, intelligent, talk-full, and spry;

And I had no need to clear my brain of sleep;
Each word that you uttered told me clearly why
You had decided to do this or that, and I knew
Quite clearly whatever to say in reply

Because all that you said sounded so clear and whole
That your words ground in like gravity on my soul.

21. May 5, 2015

I woke, awake, at quarter past three
And sat for a while and watched TV,
Then fell asleep at five-fifteen
And nearly slept through the hour I'd been
Expecting to wake, well after eight,
Because I'd expected not to be late
For lunch at twelve, but opened my eyes,
With a kind of unexpected surprise,
Closer to nine, so had to dash,
Writing letters and taking out trash,
Before I set out upon my way
To a lunch I attended so far away
That it took me an hour in the subway's sprawl,
And then, after lunch, I had to call
A taxi to visit a friend in the grip
Of an illness, and then I was back on the trip
Of over an hour to where I stay,
Then sat, for a moment's calm that day
Of May the fifth, and ate a snack
Till the clock showed seven, and I went back
To watch TV, but I dozed again
And this time slept through the hour of ten
To the very next morning at one a.m,
And then I adopted a stratagem
To get back to sleep by watching TV,
('Twas a thriller I'd waited for years to see),
Then went back to sleep and awoke that same day
At seven o'clock feeling far far away
From you on a morning filled with light
That the sun had poured down to extinguish the night.

22. May 6, 2015

It's May the sixth and a sailing sun runs high
At midday with a warmth that weaves its way
Down through the air to where the children play,
Beneath a hazy and billowing light blue sky,

Out in the open without their winter gear;
Laughters of childish innocence beset
The air with voices tinged with quiet regret
That winter had monopolized the year;

So out I went, without a scarf or hat,
And paced my vacant balcony, obsessed
With how the flagstone's edges were possessed
By weeds and tiny greeneries spread flat;

But then a sprawl of midges round my head
Drew me indoors to eat my lunch instead
And ponder once more on how banality wins
Whenever some sign of sublimity begins.

23. What Matters—May 6, 2015

Impatience is no cure for restlessness,
Nor eager hunger for a taste desired;
Verses may never glean what is required
If verses are to spring from happiness;

And all philosophizing must cascade
Into a dust from empty heartbreak fused;
And all the ideologies humans have made
Without exceptions find themselves abused;

So seize the day that predeceases death;
Climb on a monument named the Here and Now;
Let your adventure breathe a solo breath,
And let not social worries crease your brow;

For only one thing matters, true affection,
So make of *caritas* your predilection.

24. May 7, 2015

May the seventh dawns bright and clear
But doggerel drags its hobnails near
To bring me an empty downdraft drear
To poison my would-be chalice of cheer;

For here, in the sunlight, doth my brain
Suffer from splintered assumptions again,
And I fear you might think my pretensions are vain
And my hopes are so low they precipitate pain;

So, ruffled, I plead, on this, a May morn,
That on me or my hopings you never cast scorn,
For I to a terror-prone status was born,
A leader misled, a striver forlorn,

A lover improvident, dreamer defrocked,
With a free-ranging mind in morality locked.

25. A Future Time—May 7, 2015

I see the punctuate willow-drapes
Sit like sheer greens anew upon the hill,
While new-grown greenery escapes
The browns the unbudded branches tendered still;

And so did future time appear
To my scored and scar-marked bachelorian mind,
Going with whomever I met who seemed near,
But yearning for someone I just couldn't find,

And then, with a thunder-clash of tears,
And flashes of ever-reoccurring light,
I fantasized that, despite our years,
There'd be a time when everything went right.

26. May 8, 2015

Time spreads an ancient lacquer over Space;
A myriad anxious couples down the years
Have turned a home-lit longing into a race
Between desires and ever-present fears
That what was once so pleasant they had dreamed
Might turn to something other than it seemed.

27. Fresh Air—May 8, 2015

And now the greens have spread their elocution
Across the recording greensward of the hill;
Their forceful life attests the allocation
Of sunshine to the wayward weather's will;

For fresh air yesterday, I rose to keep
The windows open to let a breeze flow through
The night-time corridors of where I sleep,
Packed as they are with memories of you;

And in my sleep I heard a groaning sound,
And scrape of steel on steel, at half-past three;
A train was there, coughing, for somewhere bound,
And its broad engines conveyed their roar to me

Via the open windows, letting in fresh air
That reminded me you're far from here out there.

28. How I'll Write—May 8, 2015

Energy renders a certain bloatedness
To what was intended to be a shortened thought;
But surely such thinking's long persistingness
Evokes a divinity the Muses wrought
That deserves to be in bold and decorous verse;

My words about you ought never to be curt
Or, festival-like, be limited to days
When the knowledge that so far I've not been hurt
By you is endless cause for endless praise;
I shall resist temptations to be terse;

And that even holds for times when thoughts of you
Tend to the bland and non-inordinate;
It's then that I sift, from the glowing residue
Of hopes and longings that have been dashed or late,
Coals that provoke a swing into reverse

And castigate all temperate terms of you
As lacking what is needed to place you on
A pedestal, where I expose to view
You as an Aphrodite-like Endymion,
A fusion-beauty some might call perverse.

29. May 9, 2015

On May the ninth, you were away
When I phoned to ask if all was well,
And steely drops of thunderdust
Beclouded my mind like a tiny hell.

I'll phone again on May the 10th
And trust that tomorrow you'll be there,
And a frantic blizzard of white-ray light
Eradicated my despair.

Hyperboles all, exaggerations!
But if cool as a cucumber I should be,
Flat on the ground, surrounded by leaves,
Far too subservient I would be

For you to admire me, or raise a smile;
You'd mash me to mush, at least for a while.

30. Weeks, Etc.—May 9, 2015

To say the weeks are limping by
To when I hope to see you soon
Is what I write on a dull, insipid
And overcast Saturday afternoon;

To say the nights go by too slow
Because I'm always half awake,
Is merely excuse for explaining to you
The castles in the air I make;

But if I should say that my days are tinged
With sadness because, as yet,
We've not teamed up, might be to say
Something that later I might regret;

So I revert to platitudes,
Focus on uttering nothing at all,
Stick with compliant attitudes,
And wait for you to return my call.

31. May 10, 2015

On the morning of May, a rainy 10th,
I wanted to phone you at half-past-nine
But was scared that I wake you up too soon
When the last thing you wanted was "rise and shine!"

So I waited, uneasy, till ten o'clock,
Reading the *New York Times* for its news
About a musician who'd been to the Met
Twenty-six times and had found the reviews

Of the season's performances never were
A clean black or white, but always held
A leaven of faultiness partly redeemed
By something resplendent that always compelled;

And then I looked at the clock again,
And phoned you precisely at half-past-ten.

32. Reading the Paper—
May 10, 2015

When I clear out the brain-dust from my mind,
And sitting by TV, watch the world go round
With assassinations, peace-hopes run aground,
And endless ministrations for the poor designed,

But scattered high or low by fractious police,
Or wrecked upon a skidding ideology,
Or trashed upon contempt for law's monotony,
Or smothered to bits by greed that serves to grease

The squeaky wheels of bankers' sleazy schemes,
I grow irreverent; authority is going to pot,
Owners own less than what they think they've got,
And bright young things are driven from their dreams

By competition's stranglehold on Time
That suffocates all reason and all rhyme.

33. Paperwork—May 10, 2015

When paperwork bedraggles sombre Death,
Guilt, more than sadness, seems a common source,
And covering the vanishing of breath,
Are papered demarcations of life's course;

And you look at this, and you think of that,
And go now here, and, later, go then there,
While duties and feedings and carings for each pet
Make you neglect your wonder-lustrous hair;

Lawyers are slow, but the bills keep rolling in
Like a tide emerging that slowly creeps uphill;
They leave you no time for what now seems a sin,
Reading for fun, or eating what you will,

Or even a gallivanting up to town
To let your wonderful hair a *little* down.

34. May 11, 2015

Seated today at this table,
On a May the 11th of mist,
I sought for an infinite image
That would lend to this poem a twist

And distance it from the conundrum
That when you're not here, there's no way
To pull myself up from a doldrum
Where there's nothing I'm daring to say;

But then the phone rang! In a trice,
I'd picked it up and Thine
Was the softly sounding voice
With a quality so divine

That it blew a thousand arrows at my heart,
And all that I knew of tact was blown apart.

35. May 12, 2015

We talked on May the 12th, and then
A glow of satisfaction and of growth
Was what I'd hoped to feel; but felt instead
A residue of pain within us both;

And I want to drown it, so much do I hate it;
I want to drain its life-blood from its heart;
Not only have I hurt your confidence;
I've also hurt the tenor of my art;

So removing that residual of pain
Is what I want my poetry to do;
I want to lay a checkered blanket on it
To deaden it to stop it hurting you;

And I want to watch you walk and breathe again
Freely, and hear a laughter that betrays
Upswelling optimism that revives
And activates a happiness that stays.

36. Kicking Myself—May 12, 2015

Insensate runs the Earth along its path;
Mistakes can leave a poisoned aftermath;
I kick myself unmercifully round
A mental Earth with "too too solid"[2] ground,
Hoping I won't fall down until the air
Re-sweetened is and redolent of care.

---

[2] A version of Shakespeare's "too, too sullied," *Hamlet*, Act I, scene ii.

37. A Good Guy's Lament— May 12, 2015

This is no way I want the world to end;
Even a bang or whisper would be better
Than now, when even a poem milks a trend
To castigate its muse, its "sole begetter."[3]

When Arthur thought of Guinevere, and knew
Betrayal, with the strongest of his sires,
By the beauty he'd himself been faithful to,
He also knew the mocking of the shires.

When Mark thought of Isolde, he was bowed
By the weight of the obligation thrust upon
His tiring arms to please the teasing crowd
Who'd changed *his* realm to *her* dominion;

What mainly remains as a good man's comfort food
Is a hope he can survive his rectitude.

---

[3] The "sole begetter" is taken from the dedication to his patron that Shakespeare used to introduced the first edition of his collected sonnets.

38. An Old Man's Lament—May 12, 2015

Hopelessness is an open burning fire
That creeps, with age, to apices higher and higher,
There to outflame all hopes that don't expire;

No beacon blazes out from any hill
To say that age can outwit youth, or fill
A mind with the pleasures of favours granted still;

No mat would be spread across a carpet red
That says that I'm welcome into someone's bed
Unless I have lied or led her on instead;

No air that shimmers 'neath a tropic star
Will wait for you if I should travel far
To prove I'm somehow better than you are;

And I can only ogle a lovely girl I see
Whose dress turns out to inflame old men like me.

39. May 13, 2015

In the open air, a raucous blue
Peered through the mists of the rain-struck clouds,
Bringing the springtime to a new
Magnificence in the spring-struck shrouds
And veils of evanescent scenery;

May the 13th is this newborn day;
Its colours are more intense, its hedges
Brighter, its mists less grey,
While all along its greenwood edges
Synergies portray themselves in greenery;

And its differences from Night's adventures
Compelled my lazy eyes to stare
At Day, whose blessed apertures
Opened on floodlit causeways where
I try to play you pleasing overtures.

40. The Aga Khan Museum
in Toronto—May 13, 2015

I gaze in wonder at the shadows cast
By a high wall of multi-fretted glass
That traps the steady sunlight in its lines,
Then traces their manifold interstices
As shadowed patterns on a facing wall,
Covering its expanse with tight designs.

The world alike takes symmetry from you;
You make a logic something manifest
In a perfection conjured from confusion
In much the same way those linear frescoes, made
Of nothing but light and lines of fretted glass,
Brought panorama as its broad conclusion;

This is a place that really does exist,
Whose appeal, like yours, I really can't resist.

41. May 14, 2015

This glorious rising day, the 14th of May,
So flooded is with light non-apprehensive
That fear has flown to an eyrie far away
And leaves a world in sunlight so extensive
That happiness seems to crown this golden day;

For I can look out and see imagined You
Walking about my sungirt balcony,
A splendid representative of the view
That ancient virtues mesh in synchrony;
And your beauty is almost too good to be quite true.

42. Reconstruction—May 14, 2015

I waived what little claim I had on your affection
When "friendship" put its foot inside a door
I'd been hoping to shut to keep my predilection
For physicality with you, well, pure;

But now that friendship, wearing gloves, is here,
I'll not betray my promise, overdue,
That I will hoist the flag of friendship clear
Of any mud my motives held for you;

And on a sterling rock-face quite unblemished,
I'll engrave words for you until the sun
Turns red with envy but, heat undiminished,
Salutes, against its Western sky, a union

Wherein all thoughts I have bear yours in mind,
And you, I hope, reciprocate in kind.

43. What Hurt I've Done—May 14, 2015

What hurt I've done I want to soothe with words,
Apply an ointment's unguent of odes,
Cheer you up with parodies of rhyme,
Or serenade your life with wagon-loads
Of topsy-turvy epics laced with Time.

What harm I've done I verbally want to drown,
Apply an easy consolation's calm,
Use sympathy from my bardic universe
Applied *masseuse*-like as empathic balm
That frees your mind from everything adverse.

I want your usual self with me again;
I want to savour your wit and acumen;
I want to watch the loveliness of your face
Break into smiles that epitomise your grace.

44. May 15, 2015

Somehow a kind of winter cold
Has bleached this springtime day
Of heat and colour, though its date
Is the 15th day of May.

Nothing can ever stay the same
Unless the steps be warranted
To extricate the novel or the rare,
With news not being wanted.

But the longer the wait, the greater is
The danger that something come
That spoils what I anticipate;
I'd march to a different drum;

Delaying can be peril to potential
Friendship of the kind I deem essential.

45. Faint Heart—May 15, 2015

"Faint heart ne'er won fair maid," 'tis said.
When a woman looks for strength and force,
Until brutality rears its head
And sends her off her well-planned course
To where the battered women go
When force and strength lay kindness low.

46. Sunset—May 15, 2015

Sighing like a stupid fool
Unknowing where he's at,
I watch the sunset downward tool
As wary as a cat;

For though the sun sheds light for miles,
He knows that danger lurks
In honey'd words and made-up smiles
And couldn't-care-less smirks;

He sees, does the sun, ourselves as ants
Milling about this Earth
From start to end in a deadly waltz
To which our genes gave birth;

And sighing like a stupid fool,
He looks at me as he sets,
To remind me of the schoolyard rule,
That one gives as good as one gets.

47. May 16, 2015

Hidden among the chinks of one's biography
Are the moments that matter the most, but must be hidden;
A surface wave of achievements, jobs, relationships,
And publications should one be a writer,
Jostle to hide those moments of core truth wherein
A tiny qualm encapsulates your world.

The time I saw a woman flinch as she looked at me;
The never writing, ever, about how harsh
My fantasized revenges are; or telling how X,
Representing a nationality, had shown,
At least to me, at the time, as far as I was concerned,
Validity lurking inside his stereotype;

No, my biography, written for friends on this 16th of May,
Pulls punches wherever it can to prove I'm okay.

48. May 17, 2015

It is the *youth* of this daytime's aching Spring,
The yellowness of leaves just turning green,
The richness of the reds of copper beeches
That elevate, on an architectural screen,
Day's brilliance to an arch that outward reaches,
Obliterating Winter's everything.

It's May the 17th and bright outside;
From balconies people watched as children played
At hopscotch improvised on paving-slabs
Multicoloured to match the new parade
Of seedlings, planted in rows, or dribs and drabs,
Ready to blossom and beam in floral pride;

And even now, as I sit indoors and write,
No words I know can capture May's delight.

49. Your Best—May 17, 2015

"It's at your best that you are at your best."
These were some words that came into my head
When the darkness was thick and it was time to rest,
But I preferred to write them down instead.

But can a tautology, like the one above,
Poetic be, tinctured with novelty?
It can if it's written down to try to prove
How deeply the writer values your amity;

It can if its context starts to spin a web
That slowly enlarges, thread by thread, in size.
And never suffers a tendency to ebb,
But only to grow till, in the writer's eyes,

You are ambition requited, pliant achievement
That helps to bury both of our pains of bereavement.

50. As You Were—May 17, 2015

I love the very sound of the name of Maine;
Meaning-wise, it spells the surge of the sea,
But, monosyllabic, it stretches like the plain
That rapidly gives way to rock and tree.

And Maine was your waking-place; there you saw
The light of brimming day, and there you heard
The seagull's cries, the blackbird's raucous caw,
And the whirring wings of a desultory bird;

And Maine was your school-place; there it was you read
Stories that piqued your curiosity,
Like the princess who could not sleep upon her bed
Because to her a pea was a monstrosity;

But most of all I see you as a child
Bewildering your betters with your "wood-notes wild."[4]

A quotation from Milton's poem "L'Allegro."

51. May 18, 2015

In Canada did Victoria Queen
A stately holiday decree
When men would buy and barter flowers
For gardens yet to be;

And even more would women queue
To pay for flowing baskets full
Of flowers to cover the residue
Of winter's grisly pull;

And I feel the skyways slowly warm,
And, warming with, I start to write
This sonnet, which will take its form
From the glowing light

That, on May the 18th, today, floods down
On every floral anchorage in town.

52. For Reasons Purgatorial Perhaps—May 18, 2015

For reasons purgatorial perhaps
I slept till nearly ten
And felt like taking further naps
When I saw the sky was grey again;

For the sky can only be more blue
And the weather warm and dry
If I succeed in tempting you
To thinking "you and I";

The circling sun spins on and round
Our grizzled atmosphere,
Spinning a silent unheard sound
Of lives being lived right here,

And tempting you and me to be
Provisioners of a harmony.

53. May 19, 2015

When sunshine spills its intensity, as it did
Yesterday, waves of sunlight boldly slid,
Through branches re-ornamented and re-leaved,
Onto the arms of children who believed

That summer was here for ever and a day,
And felt no inhibition blight their play,
Because they assumed that, when it was tomorrow,
Nothing could constitute a source of sorrow;

But May the 19th dawned in a manner cool,
Dimming the day with premonitions cruel,
And later brought a rain that streaked the air
With a fearsome wind so brusque I feared my hair

Too scant to protect me from being laid low
By the cold I'd catch which meant I couldn't go
To see you as planned, and my trip would be postponed;
But all my brooding vanished when you telephoned.

54. Straight Talk—May 19, 2015

I do not wish to circumvent
Making excuses about my flaws;
I *don't* assert they're accident
Of unpreventable natural laws
Proliferating in my brain;
I'm sorry if they've caused you pain.

But I do know what I *want* to say;
I want to know that I can see
Your loveliness brighten a rainy day,
And your smile reflect a reverie
Instilled by sunlight's golden hue
Irradiant on a ravishing you;

And I've learned to venerate your mind,
Trusty and true, honest and kind.

55. May 20, 2015

I woke up early today, May 20;
I looked at the ceiling and counted plenty
Of blessings and good and quiet relief
That you had phoned, despite what grief
A-lingering might confound your heart's belief;

And idly, but freely, unaggrieved,
I put on my slippers, then relieved
Myself, abluted, and put on
Clothes for a winter I had thought had gone
To where snows stayed and sunshine never shone;

And then I saw, with unabashed dismay,
That it would be quite cold again today,
But nonetheless I sortied out to buy
Goodies for you that I thought you'd like to try.

56. If I...—May 20, 2015

If I the wherewithal had, this battered May,
To unfreeze the icy wind that ploughs the streets,
Or drench with liquid sustenance the play
Of heat belabouring everyone it meets;

If I could catch the stillness of the lake
In soporific summer-faded fancies,
And place on them an ardour that can break
Even the most auspicious of romances;

If I could catch the height of cumuli
Towering towards the firmament of blue
That flatteneth the structure of the sky
Making it overcovering for you;

Then would I be delusional, unreal,
Still fighting wars with scars that will not heal.

57. Heat and Cold—May 20, 2015

Today, from my window, it seemed so clear and bright
That I didn't even ask if it were right
To go outside to shop without a hat
Or coat or scarf until I realized that
Spring was being brought downward to its knees;
Outside, it felt like zero, *no* degrees.

Heat and cold can lead a symphony:
If it isn't you that's cold, well, then, it's me;
And if you gripe that it's too hot, then I
Can mutter 'neath my breath and roll my eye
Concocting giant fiddlesticks on how
It's always possible that we could have a row;

But then come common sanity and peace;
I like to think in you I'd find release.

58. On Death—May 20, 2015

I feel no guilt at being still alive
If, at the end, your undiminished grace
Confronts me for a few more years, until,
Like all the rest, I find a resting place
Back where I was born, in oblivion.

Thank goodness there's no memory within
Its locked wards of darkness where
Nothing is everything; I need not fear
Longing to meet you again, with your hair
Strewn-flung about your face, and you

Regarding me through a portal of remembrance;
To gritty life does death bear no resemblance.

59. Correctional—May 20, 2015

If I stumble as we talk, will then an angel
Pick me up and ruthlessly inquire,
In an angel's voice exorbitant with truth,
Whether I know I'm playing with verbal fire?

Or will instead a demon come and curse
My clumsiness and tactlessness, trowelling
It on that if once more I fumble a friendship
There'll be a mental disembowelling

Of my verse and high-flung attitudes from me?
Will I be thrown, drunk-down, upon a bed
In death's lobotomizing anteroom
Where nothing but nothing occupied my head?

But oh, my dear, I cannot help but guess
You'd *want* to forgive my every awkwardness.

60. When I'll See You—
May 20, 2015

I veer from side to side to pass the time
That putters slowly, minute to sombre minute,
To when I'll see you, newly free to greet you
With a genuine gusto that has no duplicity in it;

I cannot wait to see your veiled hair,
Tattered with grey where raven used to be,
But thick and virile with a pulling force
That leads me, in my thoughts, relentlessly

To where you are, with your smooth and youngish arms,
And figure fit to infatuate my mind;
And I must fend the dark temptation off
To ask if it could ever be you'd find

Analogous ways of thinking that of me,
Given your penchant for propriety.

61. May 21, 2015

On May the 21st it will be cold
Before the morning's cloud mass blows away,
But then the morning sun will be extolled
By merchants selling garden goods all day;

Flowers will fill the garden centre's stalls,
And potted trees extend their branchy arms
From potted soil, and fuchsia that falls
Will splay with purple ease magenta charms;

And I will try to find, for you, the flowers
To suitably festoon my balcony
And hope that you'll be pleased for hours and hours
By the music of a floral symphony

Where flowers, abundant in their efflorescence,
Of summertime, and you, display the essence.

62. In a Field—May 21, 2015

I'm walking in a kind of rustic heaven
Where fields and mud make character of you,
And the languid smell of the morning rain is even
Stronger than the smell of hay in dew;

And you crisscross the field in muddy boots;
Your head, adorned with downward-falling hair
Is etched against the sky, while languid shoots
Of muscular weeds attest that you were there;

And as you walk, your legs crisscross across
The silent field, huddled in silent woe
Because it's trapped, enmired in utter loss,
Because it cannot go where you can go;

O my adored Demeter of today,
Will *you* miss that field if ever you're away?

63. If Chance Be Chance—
May 21, 2015

If chance be chance, can chanting other be
Than merely hymning, in stanzaic prose,
The qualities and symmetries I see
When I see you in static classic pose,
Head looking wistfully up into the sky,
And your gentle hand placed lightly on your thigh?

How can a solemn, serious Art declare
It has more virtue than a photograph
When all a poet can do is loudly dare
To summarize you in an epitaph
Full of soft musics or of loud delight
That merely epitomize what you are in his sight,

When a simple holiday snap of a smiling you
Tells far, far more than any poems do?

64. The Roots of Verse—

May 21, 2015

Oh would I could be far more full of care
When I loudly stomp, in Odin-centred boots,
And sing loud sagas to the northern air,
And histrionically claim the roots
Of most men's verses lie in women's hair!

For I have travelled, with a silent harp,
On bus or steamship, bicycle or car,
To Celtic cwm or Anatolian scarp
Located near, or hither or thither or far,
But nothing sparks a poem like a sharp

Unflustered blowing of a lady's tresses
In winds Aeolian that inspire anew
A sonnet from a poet that expresses
His gratitude to women just like you.

65. May 22, 2015

The more you think you're sure she likes you,
The less you're seized with qualms of doubt;
Thus spake a book I read last night,
Before I put my night lamp out;

So can it be that I, as a poet,
Over-encourage impossible dreams
In order to fire with life every sonnet
That cries that romance is not what it seems?

And can the verses I wrote last night,
Prior to the morning of May 22,
Be only a catchpool defensive play
To stop me from feeling I'm troubling you

As a poet, because I am one who *must*
Depict my world as sensitized by lust?

66. Images of You—May 22, 2015

When I have doused my light and laid my head
On the double pillow whose support I crave,
I see enspectred images of you
Rising like an adolescent essence
To purge my memories of teenage pain,
Then vanish; I'm left with one refrain:
Unhappiness I'll purge from our senescence.

67. May 23, 2015

Sometimes events can happen so absurd
That they disrupt the real from the fictional;
On the night before Saturday, May the 23rd,
A twist took place on what is termed 'traditional':

On a super-overloaded subway car
I had to stand, clutching a bag of books;
I had to cling tightly to an upright bar
When the train jolted, me on tenterhooks

That my heavy bag might accidentally
Bump into someone's unprotected knees;
Which is, of course, what it did; I didn't see
Who it was who was hit in that tight-knit squeeze,

So had to look to apologize, and saw,
With a heart-jump, two girls, one on the other's knee,
While, like a scene too beautiful to draw,
Next to them sat two more, while a further three

Stood encircled round me; all were about fourteen,
Attractive and made up as if for a stage
On which they'd behave as if upon a screen;
Their skins were delicate pure; their juvenile age

Lent glamour and freshness to their silky hair;
Their lightly shadowed eyes were, well, inviting;
Their lips were soft, their demeanour debonair;
And I found myself invited to look one in the eye

❦ 68 ❦

Fresh and unconstrained, and I reciprocated,
While that warm lushness of freshened teenage hair
Huddled close; I felt myself elated
To a high of mental fusion, but took care

Not to pretend to even a glimmer of hope
To know a single one of them for real;
Then, 'round me they milled to get off at the following stop
With not a body-touch that might reveal

A secret hankering; no, all was right;
My chaste flirtation was the final word
That closed that drama-act of sheer delight
On the midnight eve of May the 23rd.

68. May 24, 2015

Eloquence can sigh sob-stories high
To a waiting moon who doesn't give a damn;
And vanishing unfelt into a vault of sky
Are all my queries as to what I am;

But here today, on May the 24th,
I think that even the sun feels what I feel,
Ecstatic at acquaintance with your worth,
And flush with thought that both our wounds may heal;

I woke this morning, eyes all sleepy and red,
But filled with a staggering level of high hope
That when we meet, we will be anchored
In certainties where there is no need to grope,

And in ambition's firmly rooted ground,
Treasure and embellish what we've found.

69. Permanence #1—May 24, 2015

The cherry blossom's out upon the trees;
Photographers snap them, and their lacy whites
Illuminate small pockets on the hill;
Unlike jewels, their beauty fades away,
But in a year, they're back with extra spray.

Your beauty is more permanent than theirs;
Each day that joins the slowly passing nights
Adds to the joy your beauty brings until,
Lingering, you or I will pass away,
And only what we write or draw will stay.

70. Permanence #2—May 24, 2015

Permanence is a wishlist of the heart
Given to relic'd history or art,
And if we think we also should possess
Eternity, this is a foolishness;
Eternity is mathematical;
It's part of wishful thinking; it's fanatical.

But wishful thinking burdens us while here;
Here, in our petty doldrum brightened up
By moments of desire or doom or cheer,
We forget we're forced to drain a bitter cup
If black humiliation lays us low;
Our moods are all impermanent as snow

That only lasts on a frigid mountain-top;
Elsewhere, the changing moods are paramount,
Whether it's quickly that they ease or stop,
Or fade so slowly we feel we must surmount
Pasts or presentnesses retrograde;
My admiration for you will never fade.

71. Body and Soul—May 24, 2015

When the white fever hotly does return,
But I hold back from putting smudgy hands
On the slimness of your slow-descending shoulders,
My mind is what's relieved, but not my soul;

For soul is a mix of body and of mind,
A strange inordinate entity discovered
Only when a mental mind like mine
Meets you in thought but still retains carnality.

72. This View, Again—May 24, 2015

So many colours, less of grey or white,
A lakeshine's blue, blotches of copper-red
Sandwiched among the beeches, and a sky
Puffed with clouds and dreamlight overhead:

Once again, it's there, this view
That easily pervades my visual scope
And painlessly carves a pathway straight and true
Between despair and slowly growing hope;

It's there as if a Somebody out there
Had something to say, but felt itself constrained
To keep it so quiet that only I would care
To know whatever had to be explained;

But then I'd spurn "as if," and testify
I'd rather praise good deeds that humans do;
There's Nobody out there, and that is why
I delegate divinity to you.

73. Phone-Thoughts—May 24, 2015

In the split second after saying "Hello?"
With your reply that it is you who's calling,
I feel a rift of mental heartbeat stalling;

I pull my cortex back into reality
And carry on conversing, while my brain
Spins into overdrive you're there again;

And I must imagine your menagerie
Peering and circling on padded feet
Quite unsuspecting that they're being discreet

In human terms; they don't disrupt your talk;
Their nonexistent presence in my ears
Leads me to concentrate on you, while fears

That I'll say something daft serve to inhibit
All flippancies on the phone when you are on it.

74. May 25, 2015

An early mist is heraldry for dew,
A furriness barred re-marks a mackerel sky;
Slowly the errant days go oh, so slowly! by
Before I mount the train that leads to you;

And every minute and crepusculèd hour
Serves to enchant, away from me, distracting,
The impossible draw, the pull, of your attracting
Me to you with an irresistible power;

So May the 25th dawns ever brighter
As sunrise fades to daylight, while the maze
Of Earth's activities sprawls across that day's
Impossible list towards our next encounter;

Unconscionable was the feat of Fate benign
That led me to dream of you as Valentine.

75. At the Aquarium—May 25, 2015

Deep in the brittle soundings of the sea
Seahorses drift in glorious apathy,
Whether indecorously dressed as weeds,
Or simple and pure with hardly any needs,
Hermaphroditic as they actually are;

Would I be more content to be like that,
Producing babies at the drop of a hat,
Boys or girls (who gives a jot or tittle
So long as they're healthy, strong, and little),
Smooth symbols of a parent's lucky star?

Those hippocampi, sailing as in dreams,
Have no desire to end it all, it seems;
They do not know of thwarted passions gone,
Or lingering lusts, or of testosterone;

They simply float, 'twixt reeds and rocks and wrecks,
Unknowing the inter-agonies of sex.

76. The Midges Have Gone—May 25, 2015

The midges have gone, but they've left an awful mess
On sprawling spiderwebs along the wall;
Thousands lie dead, each by Arachne caught,
Entangled mummy-like in stickiness,
Unheralded, unsung; they didn't fall,
But flew from nonchalance, to being fraught,
To dying in robes from silken tissues wrought.

I sometimes think old poems read like that;
Episodes were hollowed and embalmed
Into caricatures of moodiness,
Utterly superficial, utterly flat,
Like hollow ships riding a sea, becalmed,
With not a zephyr relieving their distress;
I turn the page to hide their emptiness;

But I don't think that my joys on seeing you
Will outlet into dubious coruscations;
I think the energy that will thrive in me
When I get to watch how you walk and how you do
Your duties will extol new perturbations
Whose turbulences will turn out to be
Poems that wax ecstatic over thee.

77. Warmth—May 25, 2015

A wind, once warm, was only memory
After a winter of dark and grey and gloom;
But today I opened my windows wide and let
Warm air invigorate my every room;

I want this warmth to penetrate right through
Each dungeon and each pantheon that crowd
The places of the treasury of my mind
That hitherto I've rather disavowed,

Places of happiness and of despair:
I want this warmth to flood and cumulate
All reasonings noxious to sadnesses
And thereby happiness perpetuate;

And this flooding (am I overwrought?) will rise
When next I see the tenor of your eyes.

78. Memorial Day—May 25, 2015

I think the greatest war-film ever made
Was *Patton,* or at least, I liked it most;
I liked the way that Patton stood to boast
He stood with Carthaginians as they fought

The warboats bearing Romans from the North;
A glitter of wartime trumpets echoed through
The darkened cinema; it felt so true
That a warrior would place himself within

A warrior's cavalcade of overlords;
A genuine mind cannot escape a crowd
Of virtual friends of whom he's fiercely proud;
They're similar men, figmented, just like him;

But I am even prouder you're with me;
You totally upstage all history.

79. Seeing You Again—
May 25, 2015

My mind is overburdened with the thought
Of seeing you again, untrapped, unfraught;
To hear the golden liquid of your voice
While inwardly I silently rejoice;
To see the lank yet lovely dynamite
Presented by your hair in candlelight;
To look at your eyes as they smile, then look away,
With a promise they'll look even better someday;
To see your shoulders and your arms so slim
No ballerina could deny a whim
To join you in a female pirouette
That magnetizes mirth with better yet;
But most of all, I love to hear your laugh;
It heals what I thought was a heart that had broken in half.

80. *May 26, 2015*

If I for you no calibrations have,
But stand unmeasured, psychological,
With height and girth unnamed and unimportant,
Then, at your age, I think that you are free
To estimate, by *instinct*, what you think of me;

You've looked at my mind and read me like a book;
You've considered my soul and find it quite controllable;
You know what I want and what my motives are;
You know of the fortress of my yearning thought;
You know my desire to hold you near-parentally,
And my longing you'll illuminate my world;

Although there be, maybe, many days between
Today, the 26th of May, and the day
When you decide it's time to speak your mind,
Please let it be decided with a voice
Wherein few calculations mar your choice.

81. Measurements—May 26, 2015

The sun is out again; it's nearly eight,
And the springtime's Fahrenheits re-delegate
Nurture to the air around the flora,
Away from the sombre dewdrops of Aurora.

When it's of hot or warm or cold I'm thinking,
I feel my heart-pulse lurch as if I'm sinking
From "huge cloudy symbols of a high romance"[5]
To a cold world where nothing can advance

Unless it be by mercury'd degrees,
Displacements that describe the growth of trees,
Wavelengths that rainbow'd colour-bands express,
And ohms that berate electric tardiness;

But numbers can ne'er refathom what I feel
When you give me permission to reveal
My admiration for your being you
In a way no measure ever known can do.

---

[5] A quotation from a sonnet by Keats, whose first line is "when I have fears that I may cease to be."

82. You Are Just Fine—

May 26, 2015

Some women need embellishments. Not you.
You are just fine, as they say, the way you are;
I have no need to conjure up a star
To add to you as jewelled retinue;

No need is there for me to call up furs,
Mink, sable, ermine or fox,
Or give you tender trinkets in a box,
Diamonds or gold or pearly miniatures;

There is no need for flowers half-angelic,
Half fiendish in their aromatic gold;
If ancestors of hyacinths unrolled
A species, new and brassy, psychedelic,

Down across eras to the present hour,
You'd have no need for even such a flower.

83. In a Field Again—
May 26, 2015

I look upon grey fields and think of you,
Bespattered by the mists of morning dew,
Walking in wellington boots across the grass
While envious clouds dissolve themselves and pass

In streams of reciprocations overhead
While you continue onward with a tread
Unmarred by momentary bouts with mud
Or twiggy derelictions close to crud;

Onward you tread, across your pastured field;
Animalcules stand suddenly revealed
By the deep imprint of each muddy boot,
And birds dive down to feast upon such loot;

And on you walk, an ageing Amazon
Who walketh on and on and on and on.

84. A Proof—May 26, 2015

Only an oldster knows how deep to hide
Unchronicled, unprincipled desire
For girls he wants to see beside his side
Who *don't* think him dirty or loony or a liar;

But do such girls exist? He thinks they do,
But they recognize the folly of their thought
And resolutely beg he not pursue
Their person, even in dreams wherein they're caught

And cast a million years away in lust
That catapults into a morass of play
Tethered by legs and tenderized by bust
To consecrate his memory of the day

When he, the oldster, proved, by accolade,
That he by nature, not a god, was made.

85. Below My Balcony—

May 26, 2015

A crystalline light illuminates
The plants and trees that lie below
And spread their leafy aggregates
Along the sprawl of sunlit glow;

I look for this clarity when I plan
Extravaganzas or overt
Simplicities for the girl or man
I seek in poems to divert;

But for you, a clearness crystalline
Must light up every word and clause
And comma in every single line;
Nothing must make the reader pause;

Readers' blockages are taboo;
Each line must have a meaning clear
Especially when I write to you,
Especially when you're far from here.

86. Troubles—May 26, 2015

Whenever a slow but troubling thought emerges
Of something running counter to the grain
Of what I feel for you, my anger surges;
I want to pummel it down and down again;

If anything acts to spoil the carefree essence
Of simple affection, or makes a trivial light
Of rivalries, or brings an adolescence
Into my adulthood, I'm forced to fight;

For I feel free to blazon and escort you;
To talk to you as equal I feel free;
I also feel a freedom to exhort you
To feel quite free in what you say to me.

87. Impatience—May 26, 2015

Does what I write have anything to do
With the fact I find it difficult to wait
To see you again, and again to worship you
For your beauty, wit, and energetic gait?

O my belaboured doldrum, dissipate!
Let Time bequeath new models when I see
You standing at the station as you wait
For me to see you first, or you see me!

88. May 27, 2015

Another sunny day; summer encroaches
On springtime's lassitude, and reapproaches,
In growing folds and robes across the lake,
The warmth of sunny Junes it used to take.

Of possibly sunny days, now there are two
Before I pack my bags and head your way;
This May the 27th sidles through
My windows, saying the sun is here to stay

Until another winter douse its lights;
On many of those summer days I'll sigh
Because you are not here, and pound the nights
With poems reeling as the days go by;

But when I go there, or you come here, the season
Ventures rapt, devoid of rhyme or reason,
Ready to hide, inside its sense of play,
The awful fact that you're not here today.

89. Luxuriating—May 27, 2015

Mine is a condensate of age's attitude
In combination with a lassitude
Foisted by you upon my stiffening soul
That guarantees I'm going to feel more whole,
Luxuriating at the sight of you,
As you fill with fullness my overflowing bowl
Of gratitude I'm exploring someone new.

90. A Storm—May 27, 2015

Tonight a storm's crescendo will resound,
Reverberating round the static hill
Which silently will stand to guard its ground
Until the storm has stopped and had its fill;

And then tomorrow will the sun arise
In a pompous splendour ready to look down,
With a somewhat saddened sense of compromise,
At the remaining puddles of the town;

I think, if ever I looked down at you,
Sleeping perhaps, or resting on the floor,
Even if it were only a glimpse, I'd throw
Pomposity and sadness out the door.

91. Helping You—May 27, 2015

I shall encircle inner worlds in me
Whose orbs are jostled by frivolity
Into an equilibrium solemn-faced
Where nothing goes too far or goes to waste;

This I shall do because I'd like to be
An older model of sagacity,
Ready to help you find what makes you smile
And feel content, at least for a little while,

To wander cultural landmarks, feeling free
Of any need to show propensity
For critical claims, heretical or coy,
That rob your world of all spontaneous joy;

But truth to tell, inside I'm not serene;
Sounds and furies linger from where we both have been.

92. Tornados—May 27, 2015

Pictures of tornados flood the screen
Saying where TV monitors have been
Filming the darkened skies that turn opaque
As wind and heat inert concoctions make
That finger down, in darkness super-swirled,
To whisk all optimism from the world.

The ruinous scores that rift the Middle West,
Channels dug deep by the windburn's stormy crest,
Lie like punctures across this continent,
Whose peoples are pure in dreams and, for the most, content,
Reminding them that randomness is rife
And doesn't give a fig for human life

But crashes down with a dark hilarious glee
To flatten everything from A to Z.

93. The Unforeseen—May 27, 2015

Yellow has spread across my living room wall,
Showing that the thunderstorm didn't come at all,
And that a sunstream, yellow-bold and bright
Has come to decorate the falling night.

Whenever distant lovers wait for an event,
Preplanned and known about, with no dissent,
Unprecedented thoughts quite unforeseen
Can come to life to spoil what might have been;

A casual meeting with someone in a bar,
A dinner where you're seated next to a star,
A coat-hook near-monopolized by two,
Someone who takes a fancy to an unsuspecting you,

All these can come about because of math:
You'll meet more people, the longer is your path.

94. A Loud and Glorious Sunset—May 27, 2015

A loud and glorious sunset fills the west;
Long barriers of orange, bars of blue,
And underwoven browns are just the best
Of the colours laid in misty residue

Across the stigma'd strictures of the sky;
Their colours are so stark and beautiful
That I hope the next two days will scurry by
Until I see *your* beauty bountiful;

And if such gimmickry seems redolent
Of spotty verses and crummy Valentines,
So what? Poets, bad and good, present
A common front when faced with Philistines

Who cannot tell what differentiates
Simplicity from the sleaze of potentates.

95. May 28, 2015

Today it is the 28th of May,
Or May the 28th, if you prefer;
Who cares what order is carried by the day?
Who cares to what notation I refer?

For today is plenitude of uphill scurry;
I've got to get my place cleaned up for you;
I'm in for a day of escalating flurry
Before night's list of yet more things to do;

But when I see your sveltened form arrive,
And occasional economies suggest,
And feel you marvel at how well I thrive
When outer winds behowl my empty nest,

Then will I semi-sink upon my knees,
Praying you'll find more qualities that please.

96. Chores—May 28, 2015

A sombre, but a lightly-fingered, dawn
Casts grey onto a bed of brightening cloud
As I awake, switching from prone to yawn,
And coffee brew (with sugar not allowed).

Today I'll get my hair cut and then shop
For things for you and me some three days hence,
And later go round and clean my apartment up,
Rounding up dust and what could cause offence;

And lonesomely discover that my balcony,
Which I had hoped would hold bouquets of flowers,
Is full of grass and weeds grown winsomely,
Victors in the battle of the hours

I should have spent on showing my urbanity,
But spent instead on poetry and vanity.

97. Fate—May 28, 2015

Improbables rank higher than do probables
For human rankings based upon desire;
The sheer improbability that you'd
Exist at all throws fat upon my fire;

And while a "destiny" founded on a star
Determines how men of action judge their deeds,
"Fate" is the fairest attribute by far
To explain fulfilments filling human needs;

So fate it was that you were stellar-born;
And fate it was we came to meet one day;
And when I was feeling far too far forlorn,
All my unanswered questions fell away

When you phoned upon that April afternoon;
I knew that fate would draw us close quite soon.

98. You—May 28, 2015

Although each hair extended down your back
Has finite greys sewn on its background black,
No whisper-hint of age-alert has ever been
Conveyed to me by what I've heard or seen;

And though, when the mirror shows you your reflection,
You see how age is marring your complexion,
Nothing averse, or odd, has come to me
Indicative of an age-antipathy;

And though, when both of us walk, we find
To going slow uphill we are resigned,
This immanent forecast of a finite end
Has never led me falsely to pretend

That age could never mar a future where
Affection must be muted into care.

99. Me—May 28, 2015

Although my face looks younger than my age,
Age has not flown me by, not leaving marks;
My neck begins to crinkle, and my head
Of hair is showing greys among the darks;

My modest beard has whiteness bred throughout;
Cataracts I've had removed; with care,
Peering down always, tempted to count the steps,
I slowly make my way down any stair.

My type 2 diabetes is controlled;
Warnings about desserts I've always respected,
And the asthma I've had off and on since childhood
Can suddenly recur when least expected;

And though I look like fifty to some folks,
My adolescent mind still likes good jokes.

100. Us—May 28, 2015

So will we be twain, then, you and I, or not?
My skidding mind leaps to a future where
You and I reconstitute a pair
Travelling to sights we'd liked a lot;

Or form a consortium of mental power
On something or other, drawings or verse or both,
And rampage over an unresponsive Earth,
Experts at being ignored but not turning sour;

Or form an easy placid coalition,
Reading the paper or looking at the weather;
If both our brains went downhill together,
The less we talked, the more we'd know fruition;

Or maybe fear will impose an inglorious caveat,
And I will stay me, you you, and that'll be that.

Printed in the United States
By Bookmasters